Unfolding Chaos

Leeshmakrishna

ISBN 978-93-5610-110-4

Published in India 2022 by Pencil

Contributors:
Illustrator: Harikrishnan C.S

A brand of
One Point Six Technologies Pvt. Ltd.
123, Building J2, Shram Seva Premises,
Wadala Truck Terminal, Wadala (E)
Mumbai 400037, Maharashtra, INDIA
E connect@thepencilapp.com
W www.thepencilapp.com

DISCLAIMER: *The opinions expressed in this book are those of the authors and do not purport to reflect the views of the Publisher.*

Author biography

Leeshmakrishna Manoj is a young writer hailing from Delhi. She has her works published in more than 10 books. She began writing at the age of 10 and the creativity has spurred since. Her poems are inspired by the incidents around with a tint of flowy words.

CONTENTS

Epigraph

Each and every work you see here is a spontaneous rush of adrenaline.

Just kidding.

Everything you see here is a pure depiction of myself. Of my reflection. Of how I feel. Of my true self. None of the feelings portrayed here is fake. Everything happens for a reason and so did this. With this emotional start, let's begin; Unfolding the Chaos.

Acknowledgements

Thanks-
To my parents;
who supported me throughout.
To my brother
To my friends
To the universe.

Introduction

A)POEMS and MICRO TALES-

B)ESSAYS-

1. No More

They stopped by the bridge,
for some fresh air.
A mile away stood a man.
Armoured he was, with a smile.

'Where do you live?'
They asked him.
'Well, sir,
We did.

Right below where we stand.'
A breeze bristled their bare arms.
The air was fresh no more.

2. Love Undefined

'But what if you never feel anything for him, ever. He's not yours, darling…'
'I will, if I choose to.' she said.

With tears in her eyes, she signed the adoption papers.

3. Because of You

The day I'd never wish for,
the day I'd never seen though.
It's like a nightmare coming closer,
and life is getting uglier .

We met as strangers,
we came closer.
Neither I ,nor you knew,
that this day had no clue.

It was our worst fear,
that came very near.
We've lived for this hour,
and life became a bit sour.

We though never fought,
but that was apparently,
the way we thought.

4. Poison of Love

He lied on the floor,
gasping for his dying breath.

In a corner of their four-year apartment,
filled with the pictures of their undying love,
she stood, with poison in her hand.

Poison of love, she'd call it.

5. Her

That day was mild,
when the class was quiet.
I wonder how they tried,
alienating from the wild.

She gets into every grave concern,
They would rather stay away from.
She corrects the worst pages,
'Cause she is meant to from ages.

'We'll miss you.' said they,
on the last departure day.
Never did they realise,
She was a boon from heaven.

6. ILY3000

'I love you 3000, dad.'
'3000? Beta, I love you ∞.'

For the trends outdated,
his 15 year old love.

7. To The Moon and Back

Time flies and days pass,
Rain dews and water showers.
Yet the human heart stood cold,
To the rivalries who once stayed bold.

Hands stayed numb,
while the brain did the work.
As many as a hundred lives lost,
Yet humanity in the darkness lurked.

Amid the wearisome times,
 Love takes a hard turn,
For the Moon and back remained,
A theory to never look for.

8. Beauté de la Nature

I could go miles,
And see the wide smiles.
Of the people who won hearts,
Whose stories were a work of art.

It was indeed a melodious evening,
The crescent moon above just like a bow,
With stars around,
and planets in a row.

Ah! The nature decided today,
Under the pale moon we lay,
With bare arms and a hazy day,
The vibe paved the way.

9. Is it Worth It

Death is not the answer to every question,
Death is not what you wish.
Death is what comes in sensation,
And goes like a swish.

Fight to who you believe,
Though 'tis better to grieve.
The sands of life are to go,
So fight with an arrow and bow.

The hand is to donate,
To a handless mate.
The eyes are to see,
To the one who is me.

Death may bring you happiness,
But the feelings of the beloved,
Are endless…

10. God's Own Country

When the sun shuts its eyes,
The moon waking up to rise …
The dreamy creamy night to start,
A holiday to the stars.

I wish I could be one of those,

The ones who see the dawn .
And that's the point where we meet,
The god's own country's feet.

I wish I could be one of those,
The ones who see the dawn .
And that's the point where we meet,
The god's own country's feet.

The Kathakali portraying the state,
And Payasam being the luscious.
With every mile of ours,
will we find a malayalee another.

11. Unheard

Lending ears to a solus teenager,
Away from any look of danger.
With her eyes filled; there she stood,
I felt her silence meant no good.

She seemed unheard,
She was nearly blurred.
Of all her dabbles one by one.
For little was she cared by anyone.

She is quiet; numb; and clear
But slowly did nobody see.
Her presence never was dear,
For seldom was she with glee.

She is there,
But you don't see.
She was done a little unfair,
For not one heard her silent plea.

She wished she mattered,
as her voice leisurely shattered,
Among the heard voices she stays,
Held back by the unheard days.

12. To the One's Who Complete Me

I am not someone,
Who vents to my friends.
But I have done to you,
I am pretty sure.

I am not someone,
Who console.
But I have done to you,
I am pretty sure.

I am not someone,
Who smiles at people.
But I have done to you,
I am pretty sure.

I am not someone,
Who writes poems about people.
But I have done for you,
I definitely have.

13. Version

To the younger version of mine,
I've grown into someone just fine.
To the future version I got to see,
I hope I'll make you the best version of me.

14. Ideally Existing

Oh how I wish I was there,
With smiling hands and glowy eyes.

Oh how I wish I was there,
Among the happiness, one can ever feel.

Oh how I wish I was there,
With my eyes never tired.

Oh how I wish I was there,
Among the ones who never cry.

Oh, I really wonder if,
Do souls like this exist for real?
For happiness and misery come and go,
Like a little leaf in a river flow.

15. Rugged Hands

His hands were blue with the ink he spilled,
The letter spoilt;
And memories killed.

With a heavy heart,
He began to jot again,
His broken love,
for a soul apart.

16. Recall

Do you recall the first time,
You stood up,
and then fell down,
Because, 'up' was too high?

Do you recall the first time,
You tried speaking,
But were stopped,
Because, not 'every' voice matters?

Do you recall the first time,
You spoke for the truth,
But were told to lie,
Because 'truth' apparently hurts?

I'm sure you recall the first time,
You held a pen and wrote,
and didn't stop,
Because 'writers' don't stop.

17. Vision Foreseen

I wake up to a dizzy ray of sunlight,
with a new beginning in sight.

For numbers may go up and down,
there exist other worries in town.

I dream of a vivid nation,
with those little worries not in vision.

Of little ones looking at their books; not the garage nooks.
Of women working for themselves; not for the untidy shelves.
Of farmers with sales upsoar; not their bodies on the shore.
Of teachers and doctors with their pride; not the merciless hide.
Of mental health seen in the light; not people scared to fight.

Of a day much bright,
my soul feels it's just right.

18. Their Love

I peeped into my loved ones hearts,
For the place is filled with utter love.
I swayed my clear way,
through the path of love.

The fights we had,
The distance we shared,
Never could explain the love we paved.
Ah! the motherly love it held.

Never can I ever tell you,
the beauty that they held within.
But for a fact I can begin,
That their love was never blue.

19. A Letter I Can Never Stop Loving

Dear 17 year old soul,
Probably looking at this in the future, I am going to laugh it off. But anyways, it isn't a pleasant time. With the virus around and exams on the shoulders, the pressure's real heavy. But everything comes to an end. Be it happiness or moments in pain. But it is upto us how we handle those situations calmly and do not let it affect us. To move forward in patience, for the patience will be fruitful.

Apart from that, I turned 17 a few days ago, and I cannot believe I am 1 year close to turning an adult. 17 years of handling pain, happiness, guilt, regret and what not. All these years, it was always about living for the next best moment that is to come. 'Oh, I got a 100 subscribers. 200 must be a charm!', 'Oh, I got 1k views on the first reel, 10k must be great!'. I never lived in the moment. To celebrate what is there and not what is yet to come because it's not necessary the future may be pleasant but the present is right? As much as cliché as this might sound, to celebrate the moment I currently float in, is something I'd persist to do!

20. What is Love, really.

First love is a delicate one. Something you never want to let go at that moment. A bond that will hurt real bad if broken. If I was to mention my first love ever, it was my mind. Art, books, literature occupied my crowded mind at a very young age and it wouldn't be wrong to mention that my first love were these pretty amazing things to ever exist. The best part? They're still with me; for the rest of my life. A person may come and go but these can never. Yes, to talk to someone, a real person is good. But lending ears to hundred other stories written, meaningful art pieces, and love stories are better. From my very first hand at drawing to my first ever novel completed, they proved how love doesn't need to be a person. My love for them will never die and its a promise I make.

Lastly,
books, poets, colours and line,
are the things I can forever call mine.

21. Perspective I Hold

When a kid, I always thought of having a lot many friends, a big villa to reside in, lots of chips in hand and what not. Honestly, who hasn't dreamt of all the unimaginable things in their lives? Well, times have changed. My mind has evolved into something young Leeshma could never have thought of. Today if I am asked of Life; in my perspective, it's about the tiny little moments and people in your lives, and definitely not the chips you wanted. It has always surprised me of how people remain in each other's memories for years and aren't even aware of. Of people hugging each other after a long day of work. It may not mean literally anything to us. But to them, it's a magical momeny they lived for the entire day. They have something others don't and they are pretty grateful about it. Similarly, many of us have a billion of things to live for. Things which only we can realise the worth for. And if life was to live for those little moments and creatures, isn't life something to cherish for every moment? Of course it is.
Well, sitting under a tree on a sunny day, with my bestfriend, will I reminisce the weird and embarassing things we did together, is a perfect day I could say.

Afterall,
things you love you live for,
for Life can be any folklore.

22. What Really Matters

Well, the one thing I want to believe in at this point in her life? Probably the fact that things eventually come to their place if they are meant to be. Everything happens for a reason and if the happening was devastating, it's probably because it was meant to be. To be able to overcome such drowning moments in your life is the one thing you can be utterly proud of. It's not like the moment is going to last forever. Yes, the current times are hard and seem unending while everything around you starts to break out. But it will fall into place. Maybe someone up there wishes you become stronger and stronger every moment. Mate, what is a life without hurdles? If the path was to be easy everytime, what is it that you can be proud of then by the end of the day?

Lastly,
Hurdles will come and go;
but the victor is the one who is up even when low.

Notes

The End.

www.ingramcontent.com/pod-product-compliance
Lightning Source LLC
LaVergne TN
LVHW050429160726
843469LV00041B/1293
9789356101104